CHRISTMAS CHARM

ADULT COLORING BOOK

By

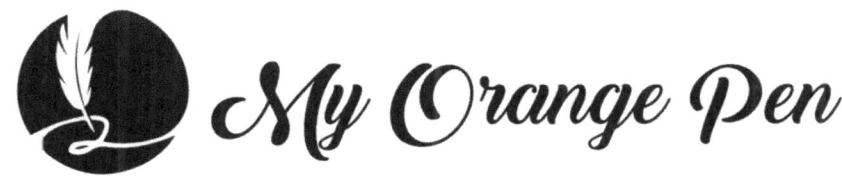

The beauty and splendor of Christmastime abounds in this heartwarming collection of 25 delightful drawings easy to be filled with reds, greens, and other bright colors befitting the season.

Once you have completed all of them don't forget to check the last page to get your FREE extra 15 drawings!

Copyright © 2020 My Orange Pen

All rights reserved. No part of this publication may be reproduced, distributed, or transmitted in any form or by any means, including photocopying, recording, or other electronic or mechanical methods.

ISBN: 9798560431020

COLOR TEST PAGE

Page intentionally left withe

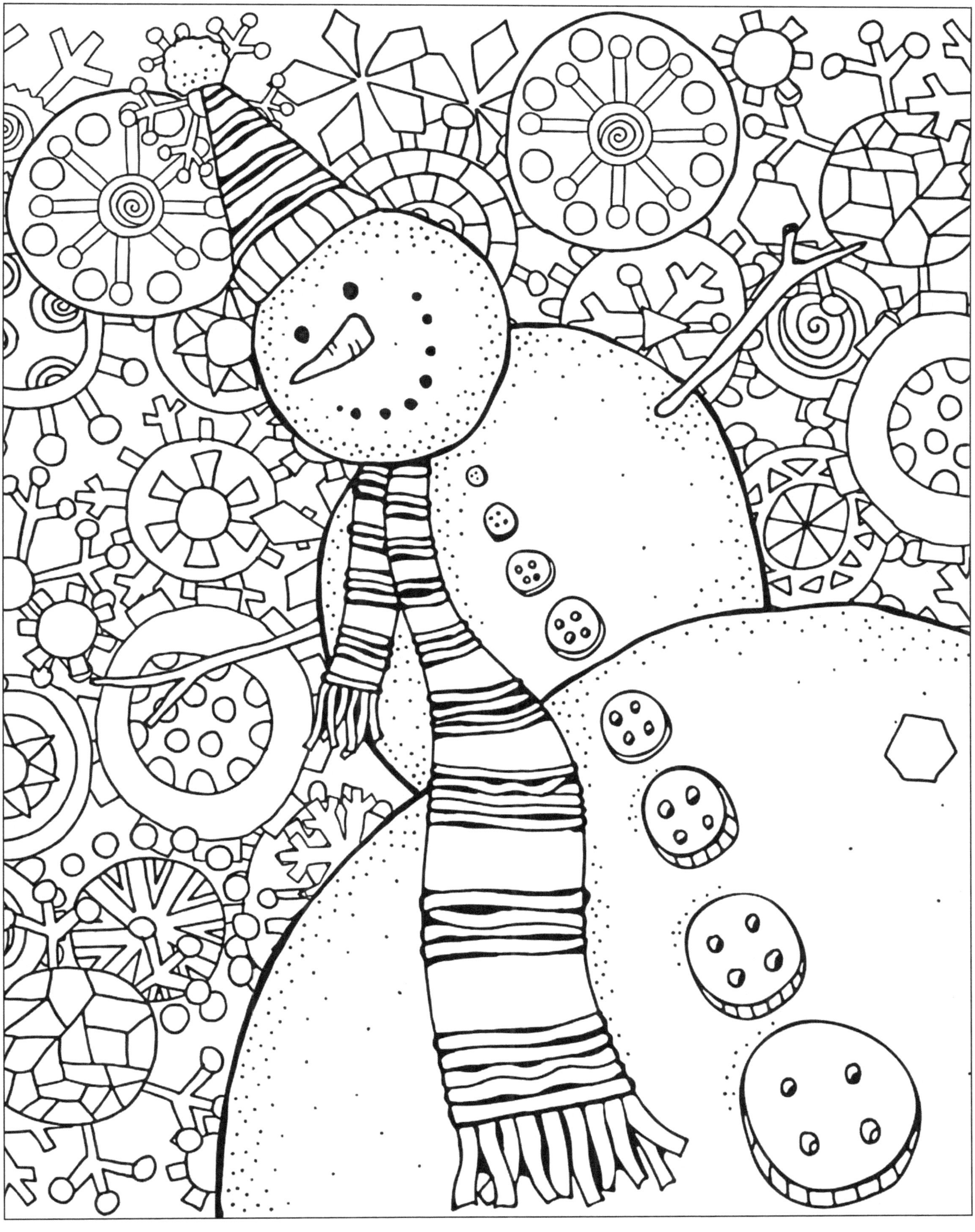

CHRISTMAS CHARM |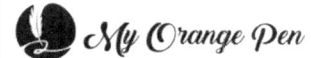

CHRISTMAS CHARM

Page intentionally left withe

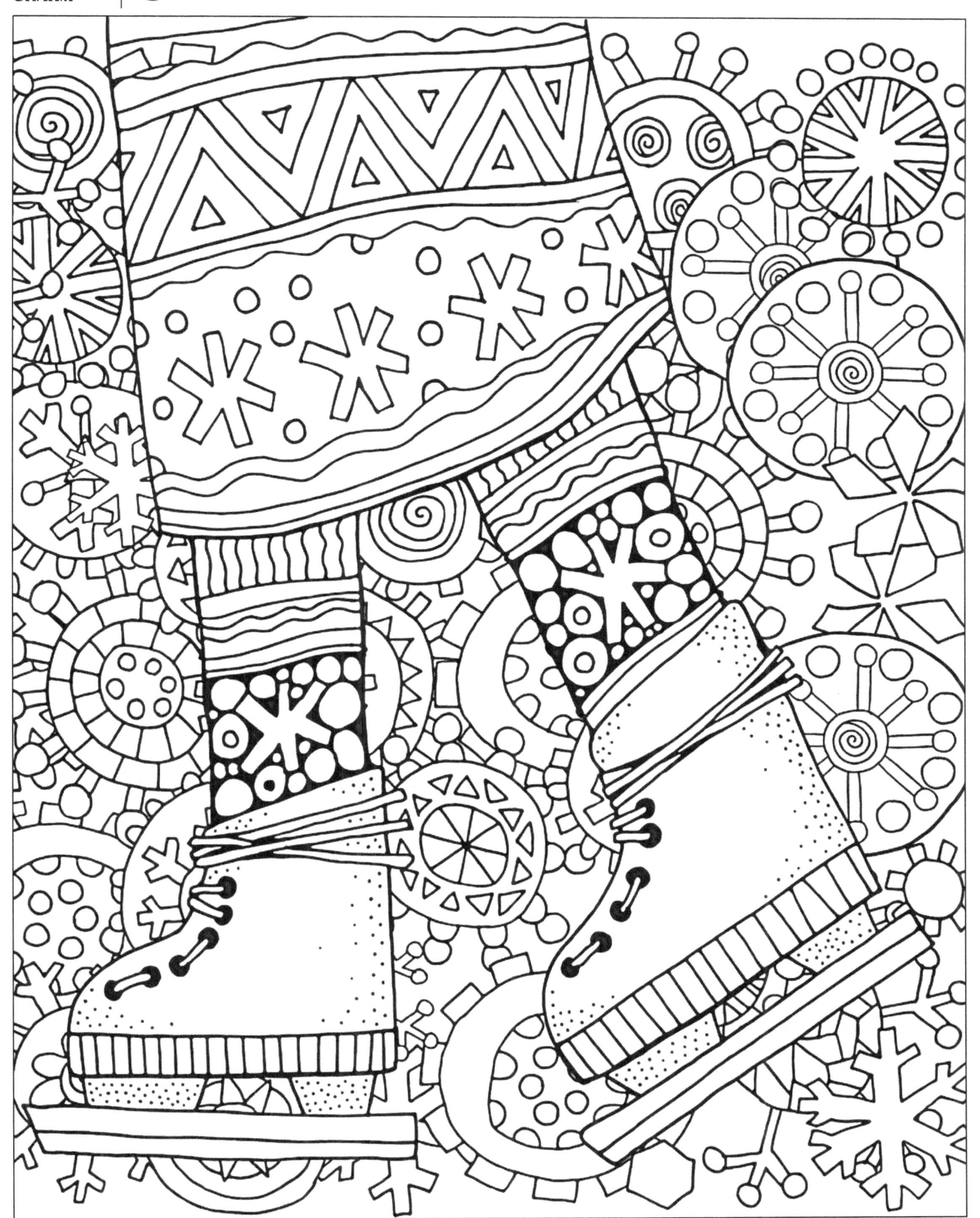

CHRISTMAS CHARM

Page intentionally left withe

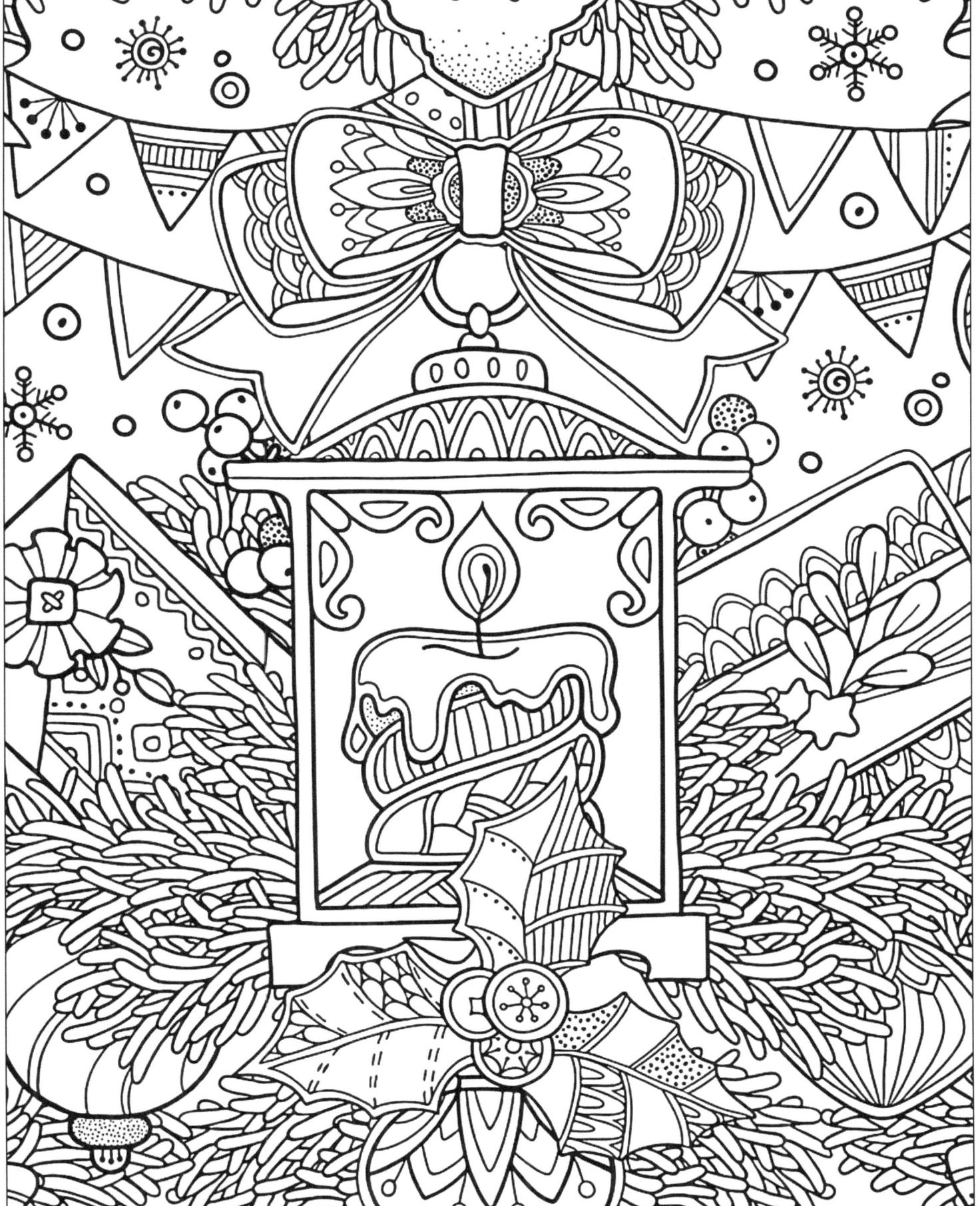

Page intentionally left withe

CHRISTMAS CHARM | My Orange Pen

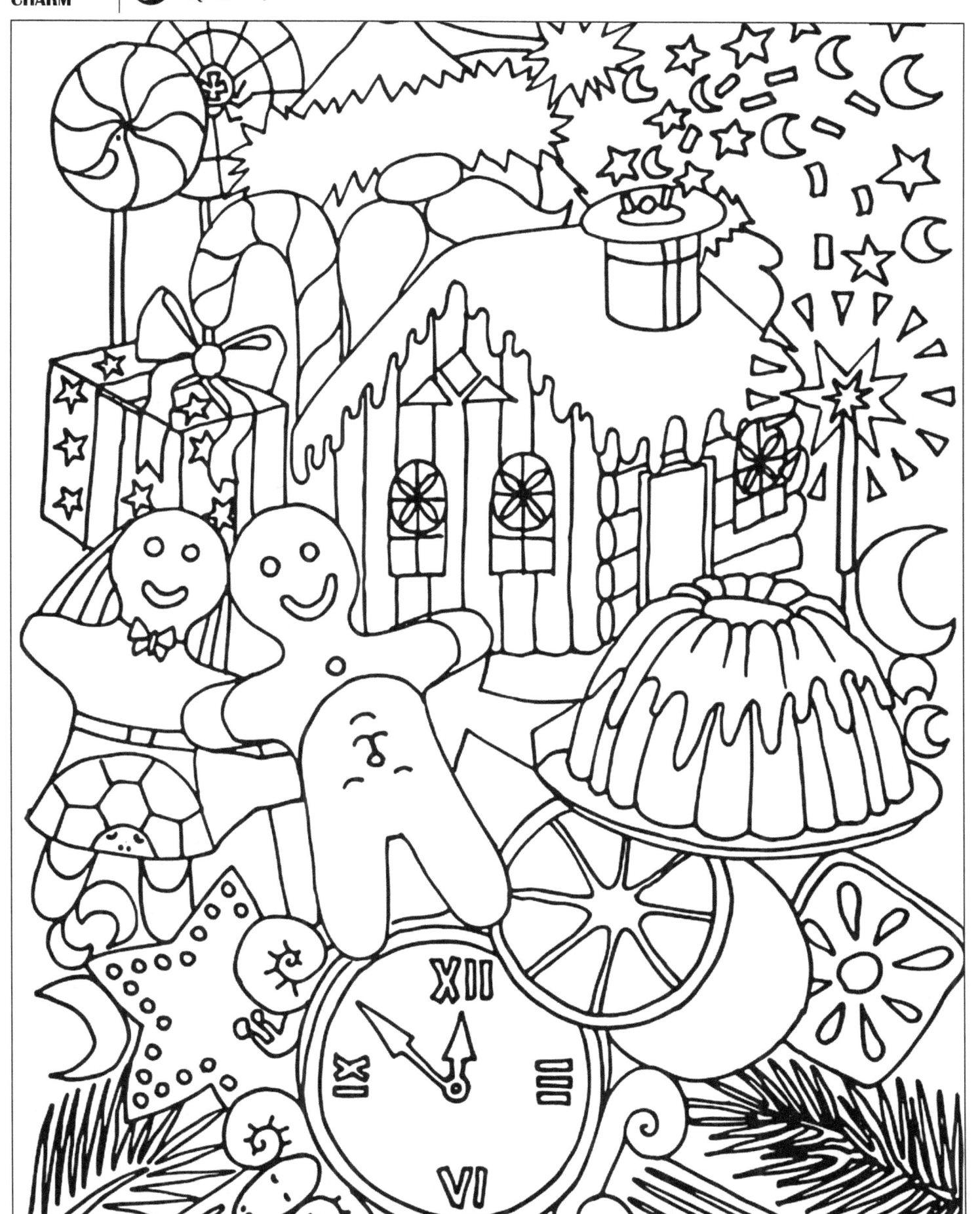

Page intentionally left withe

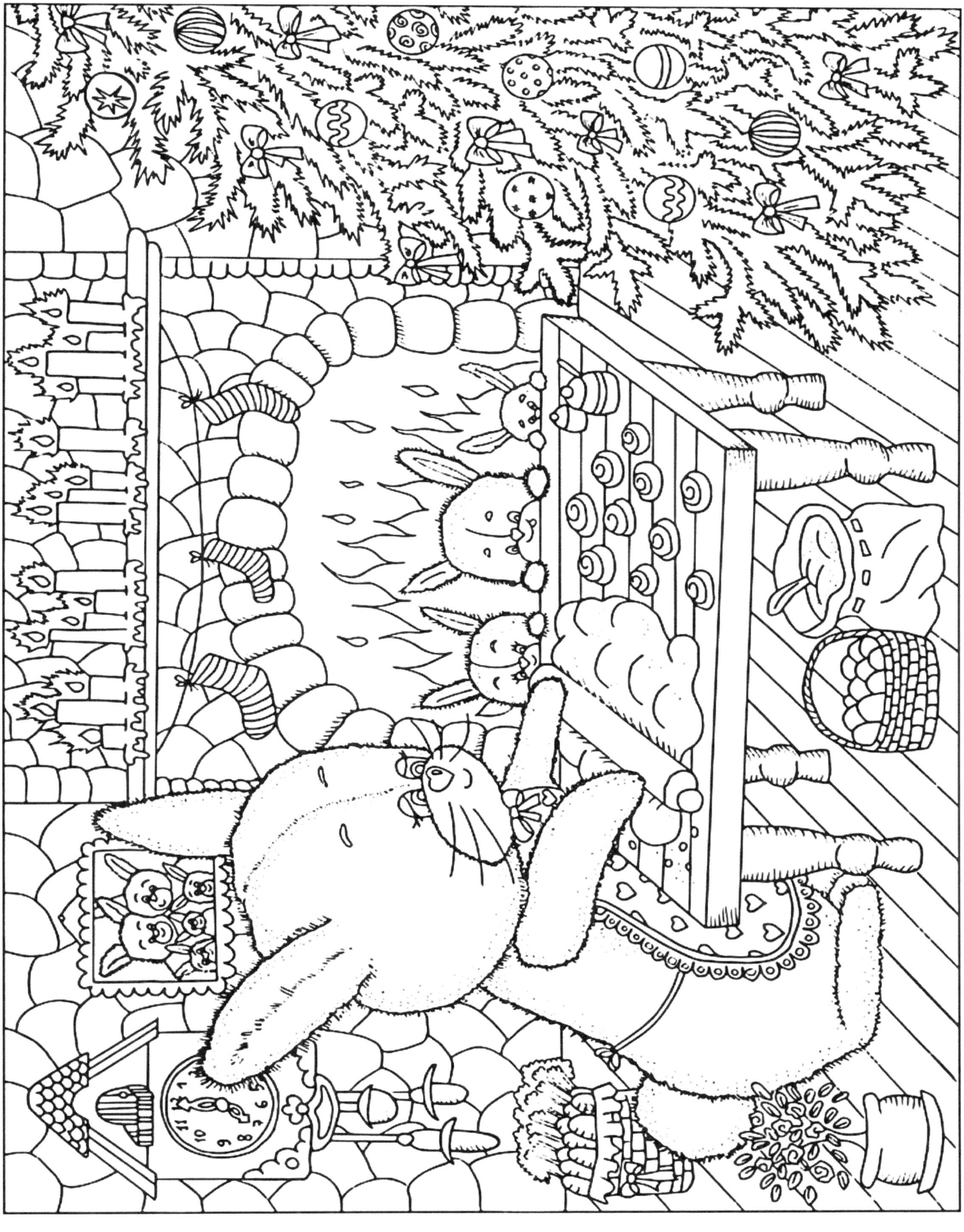

CHRISTMAS CHARM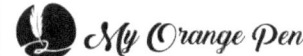

CHRISTMAS CHARM

Page intentionally left withe

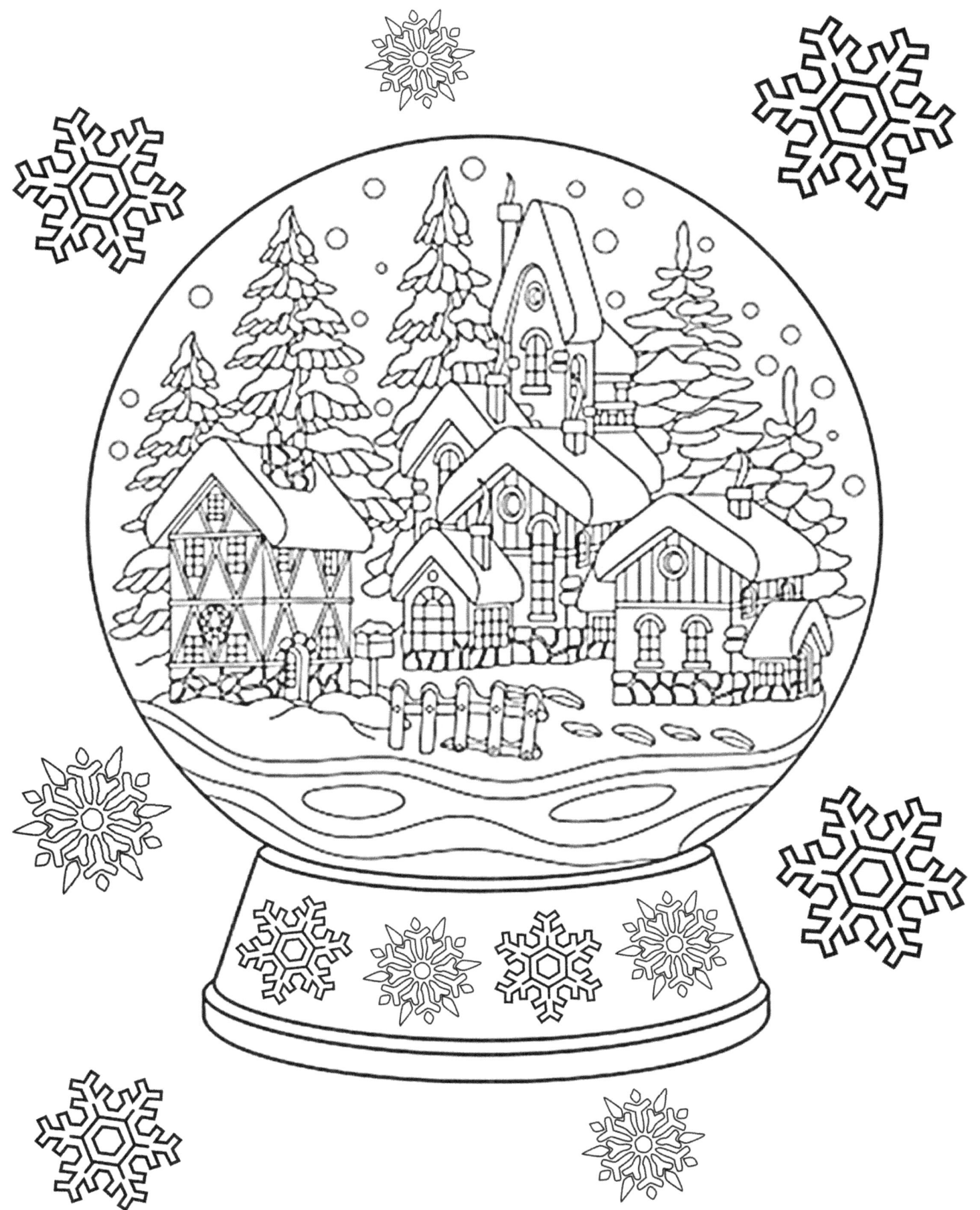

CHRISTMAS CHARM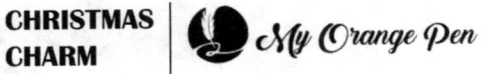

Page intentionally left withe

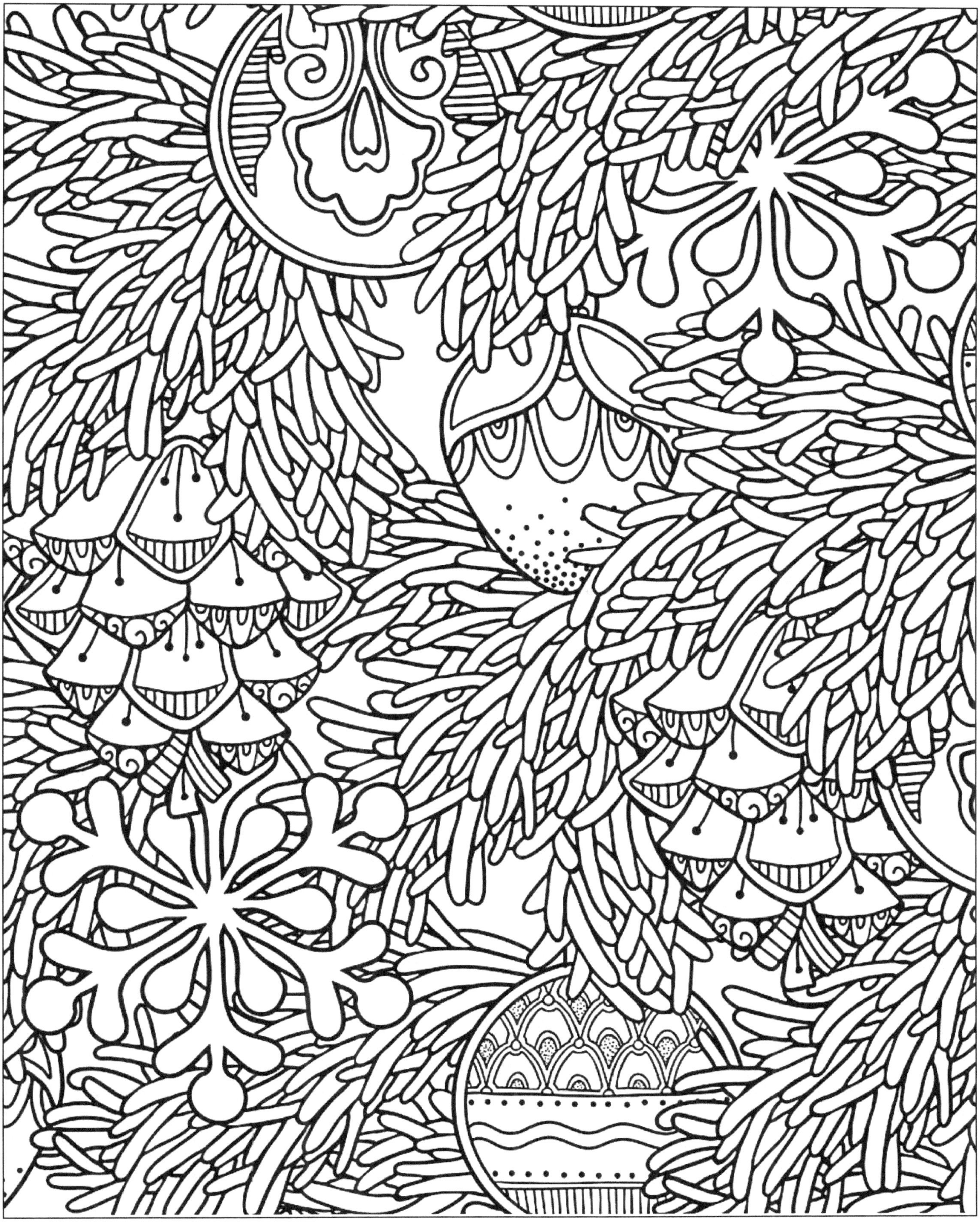

CHRISTMAS CHARM | My Orange Pen

Page intentionally left withe

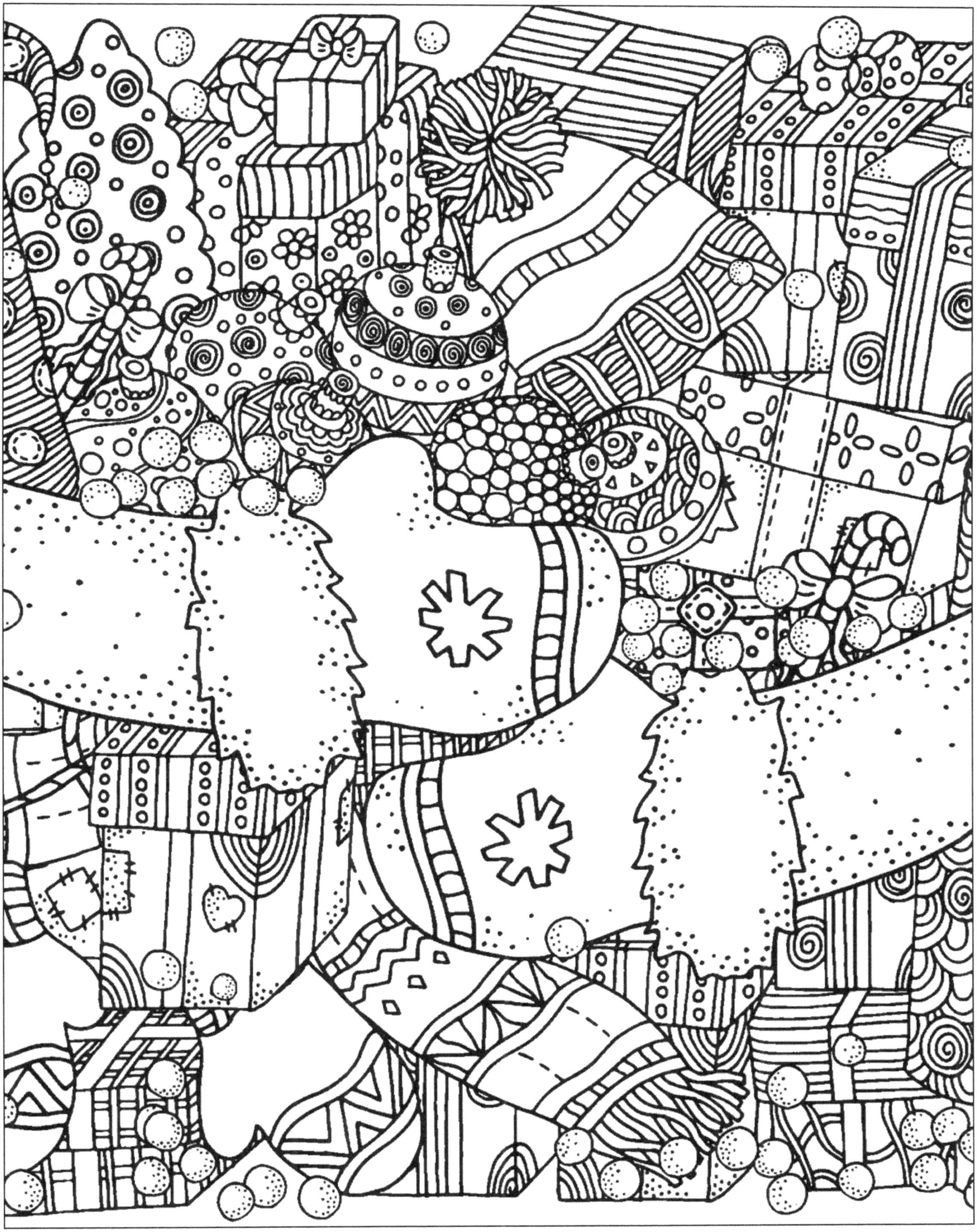

CHRISTMAS CHARM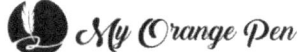

CHRISTMAS CHARM | My Orange Pen

Page intentionally left withe

CHRISTMAS CHARM | My Orange Pen

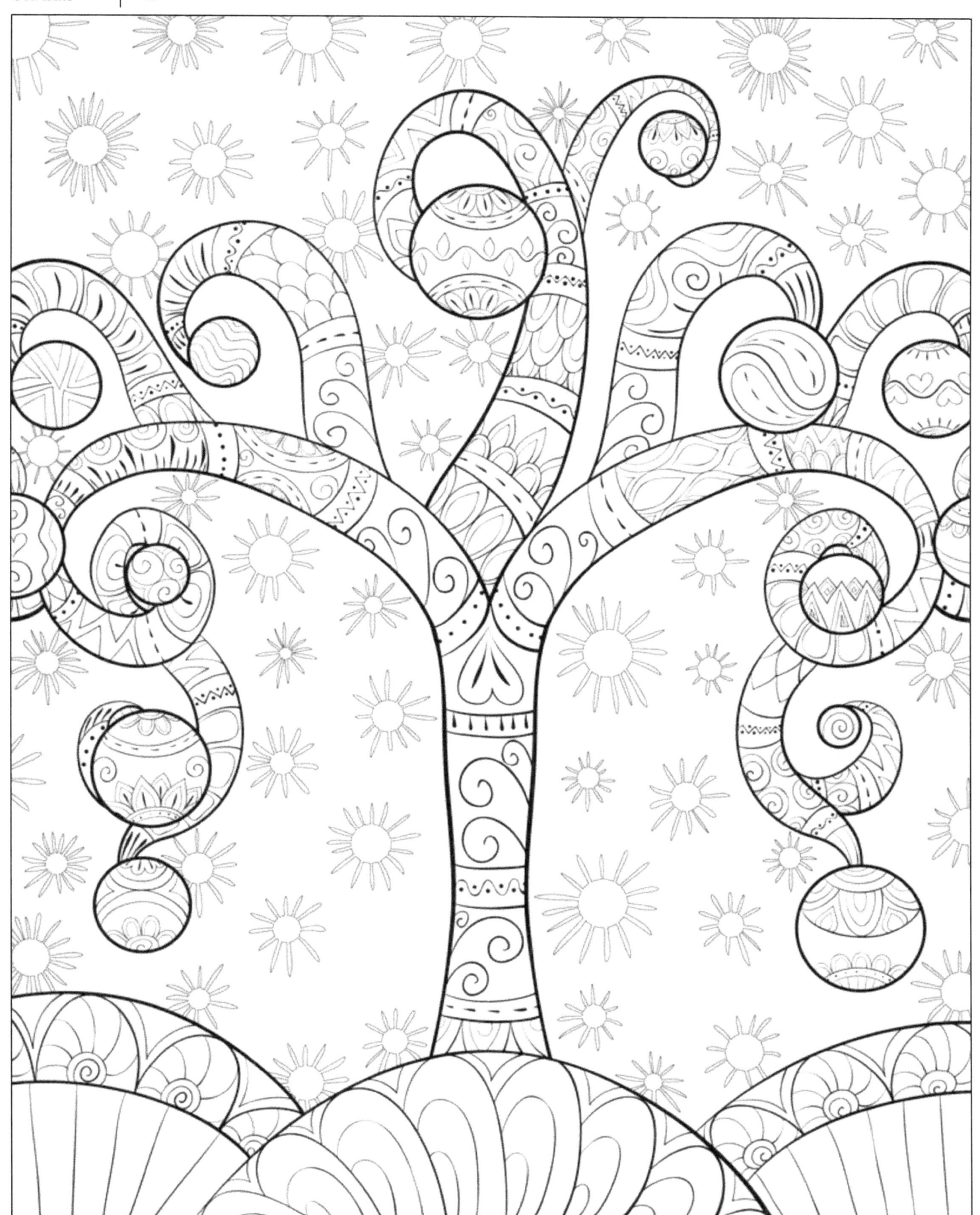

CHRISTMAS CHARM |

Page intentionally left withe

CHRISTMAS CHARM

My Orange Pen

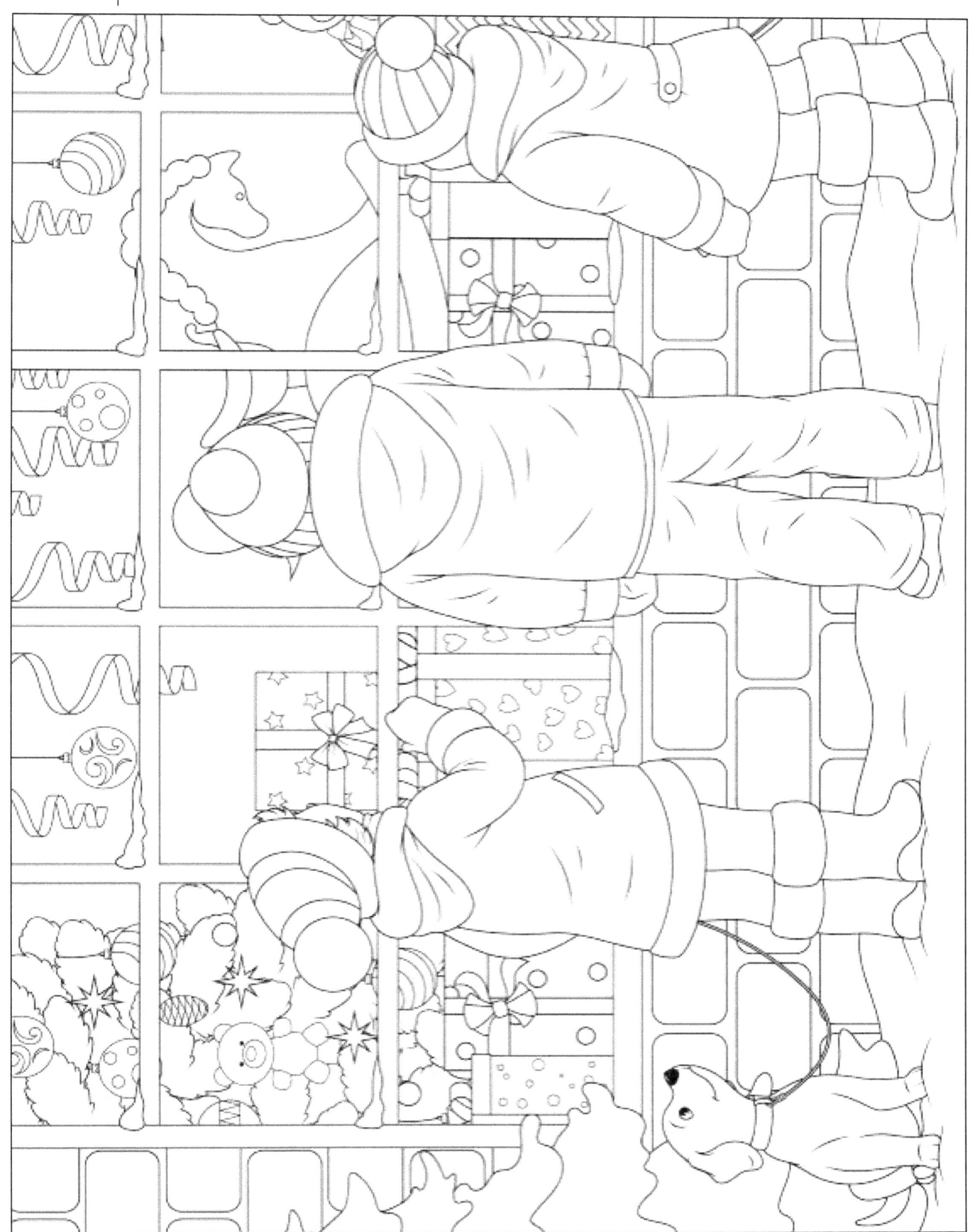

CHRISTMAS CHARM

Page intentionally left withe

CHRISTMAS CHARM | *My Orange Pen*

Page intentionally left withe

CHRISTMAS CHARM | *My Orange Pen*

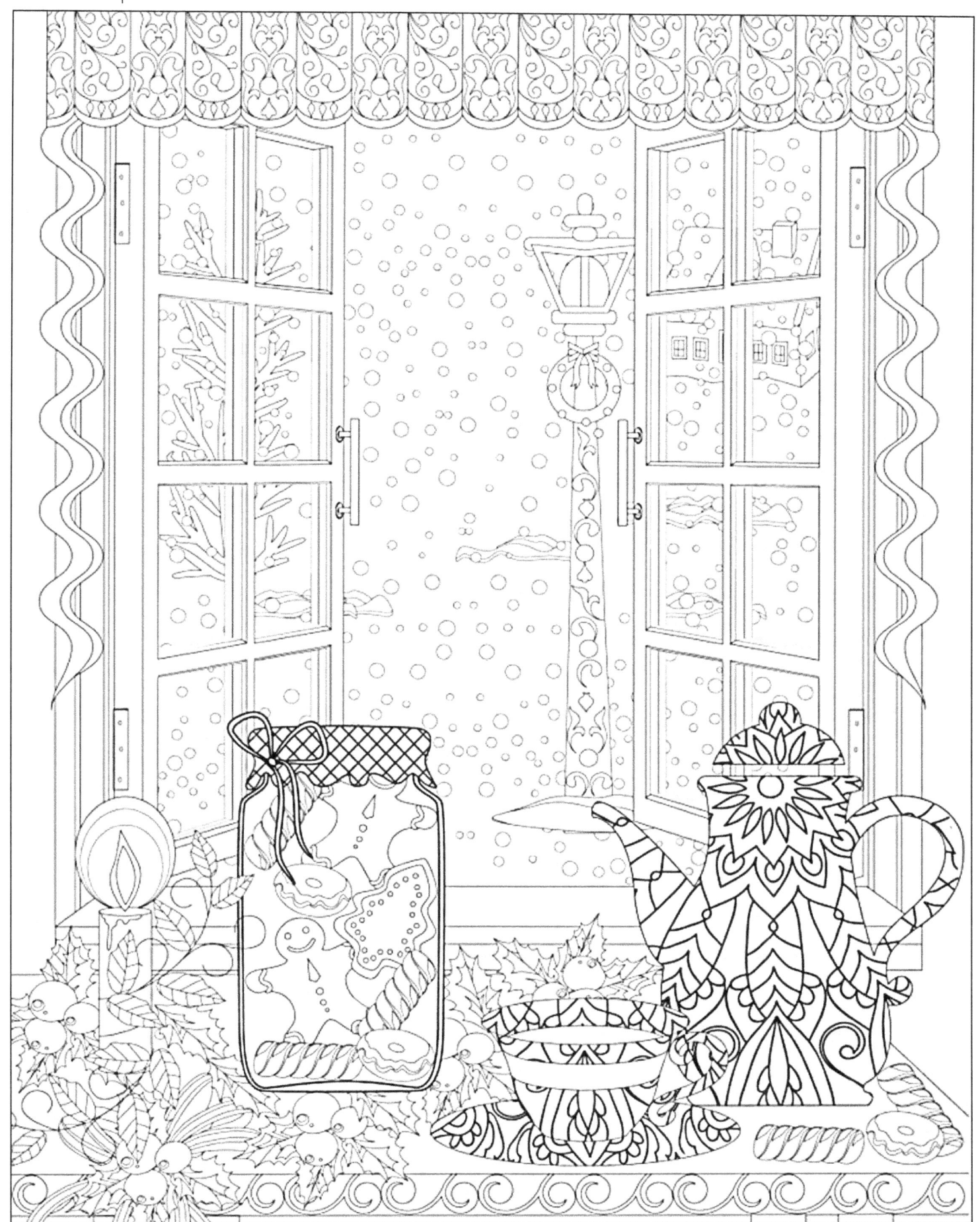

Page intentionally left withe

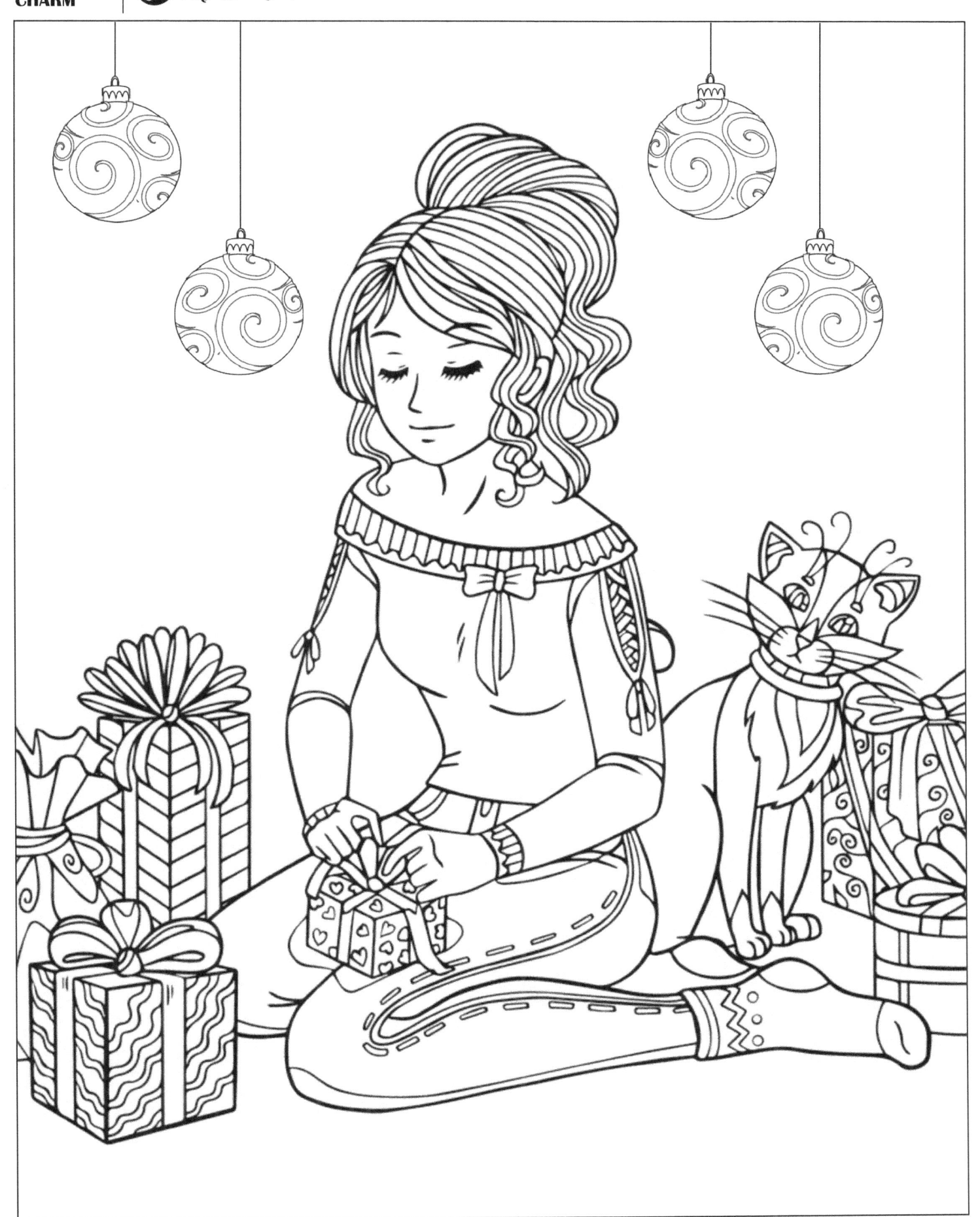

Page intentionally left withe

CHRISTMAS CHARM | My Orange Pen

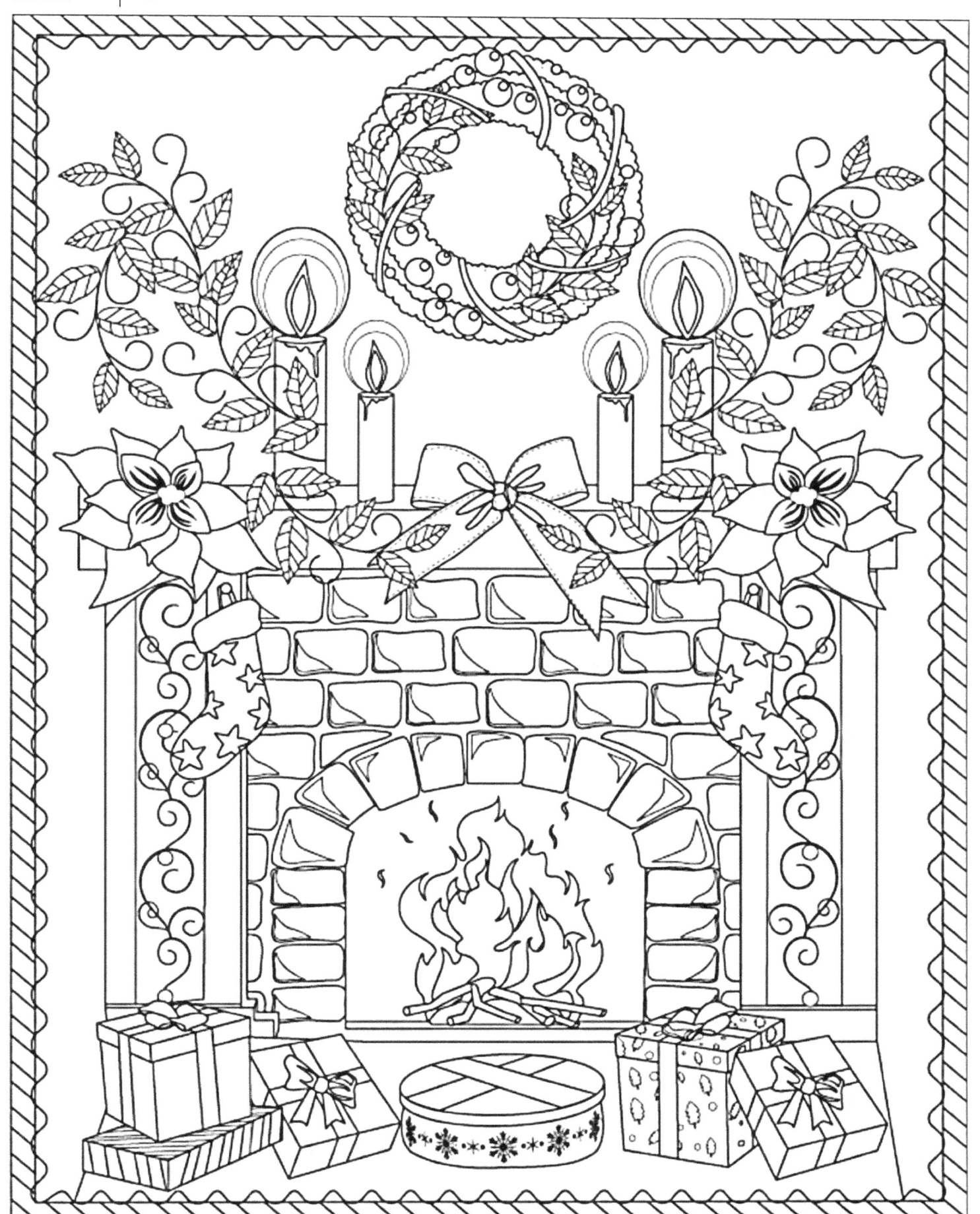

Page intentionally left withe

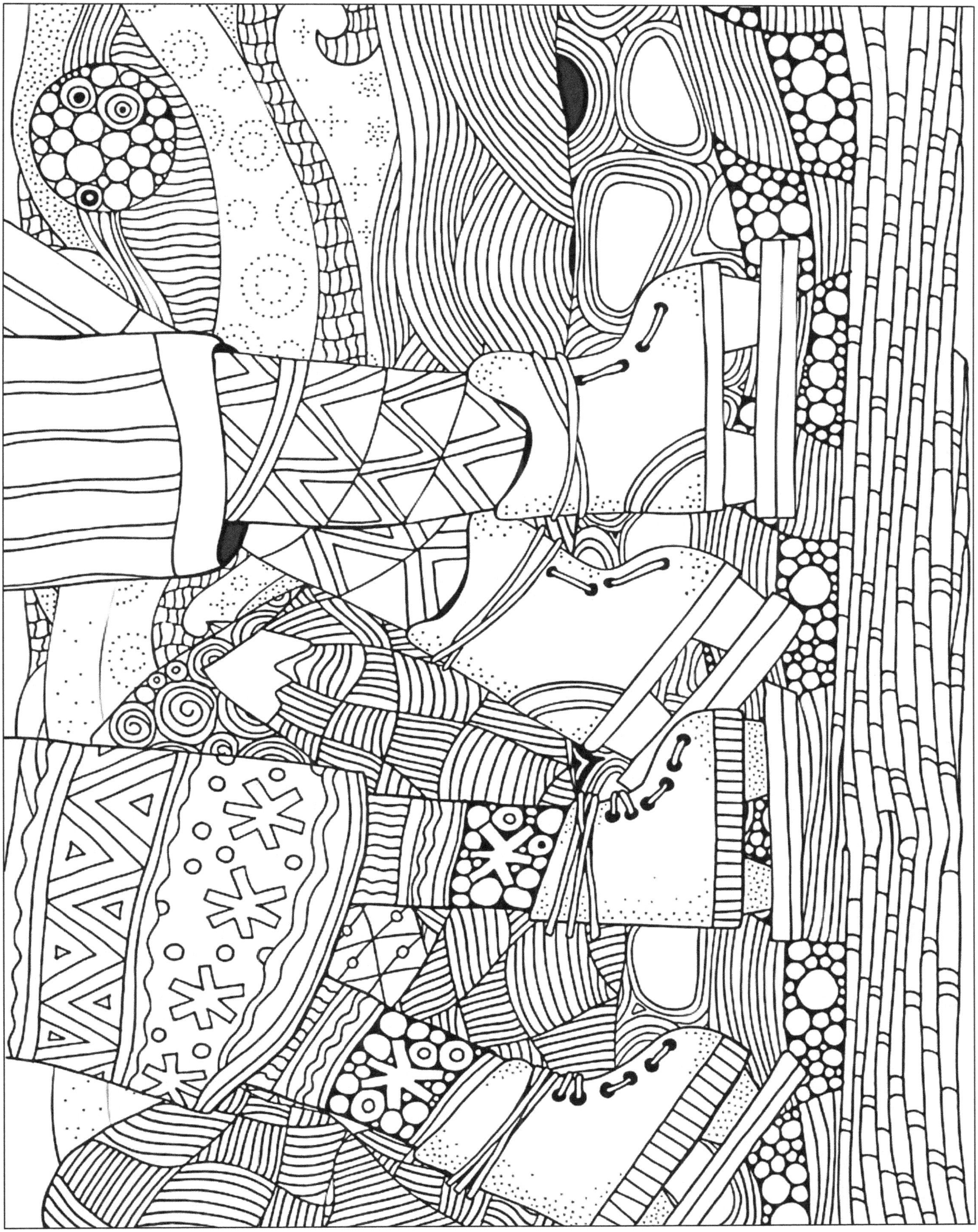

CHRISTMAS CHARM

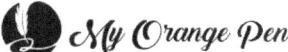

CHRISTMAS CHARM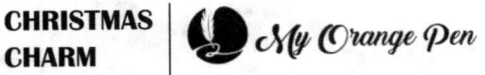

Page intentionally left withe

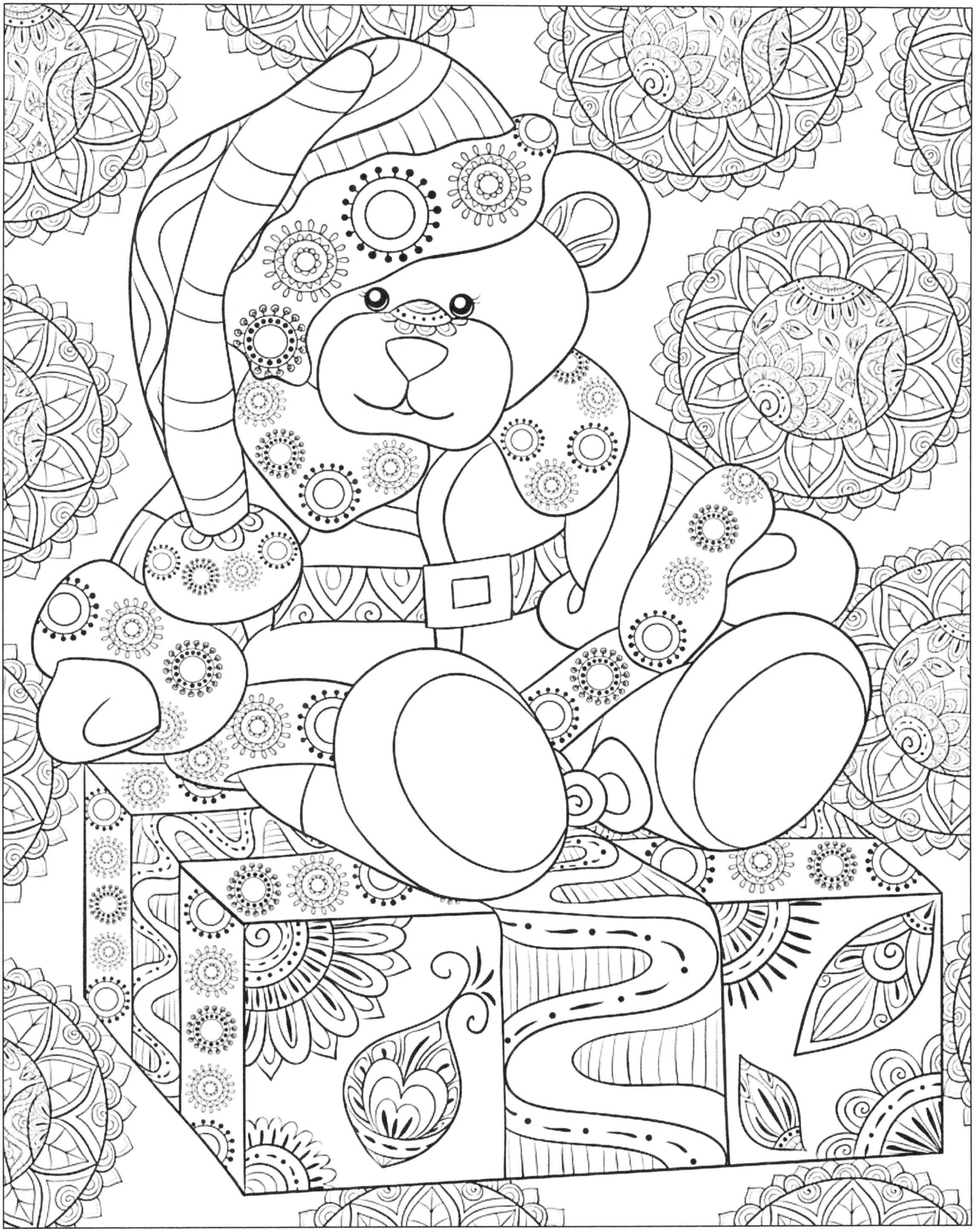

CHRISTMAS CHARM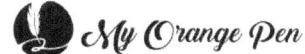

Page intentionally left withe

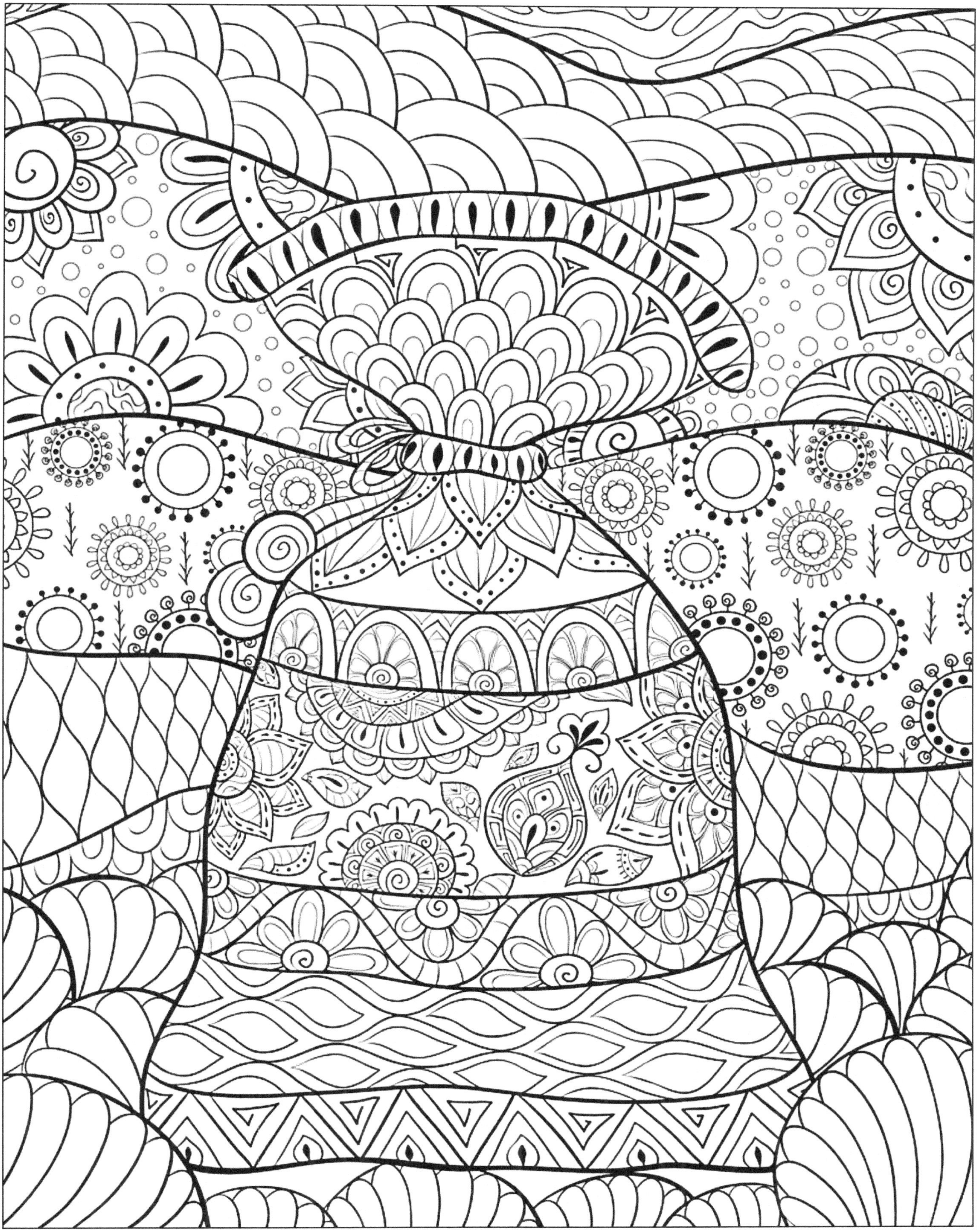

CHRISTMAS CHARM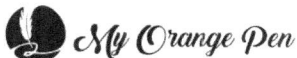

Page intentionally left withe

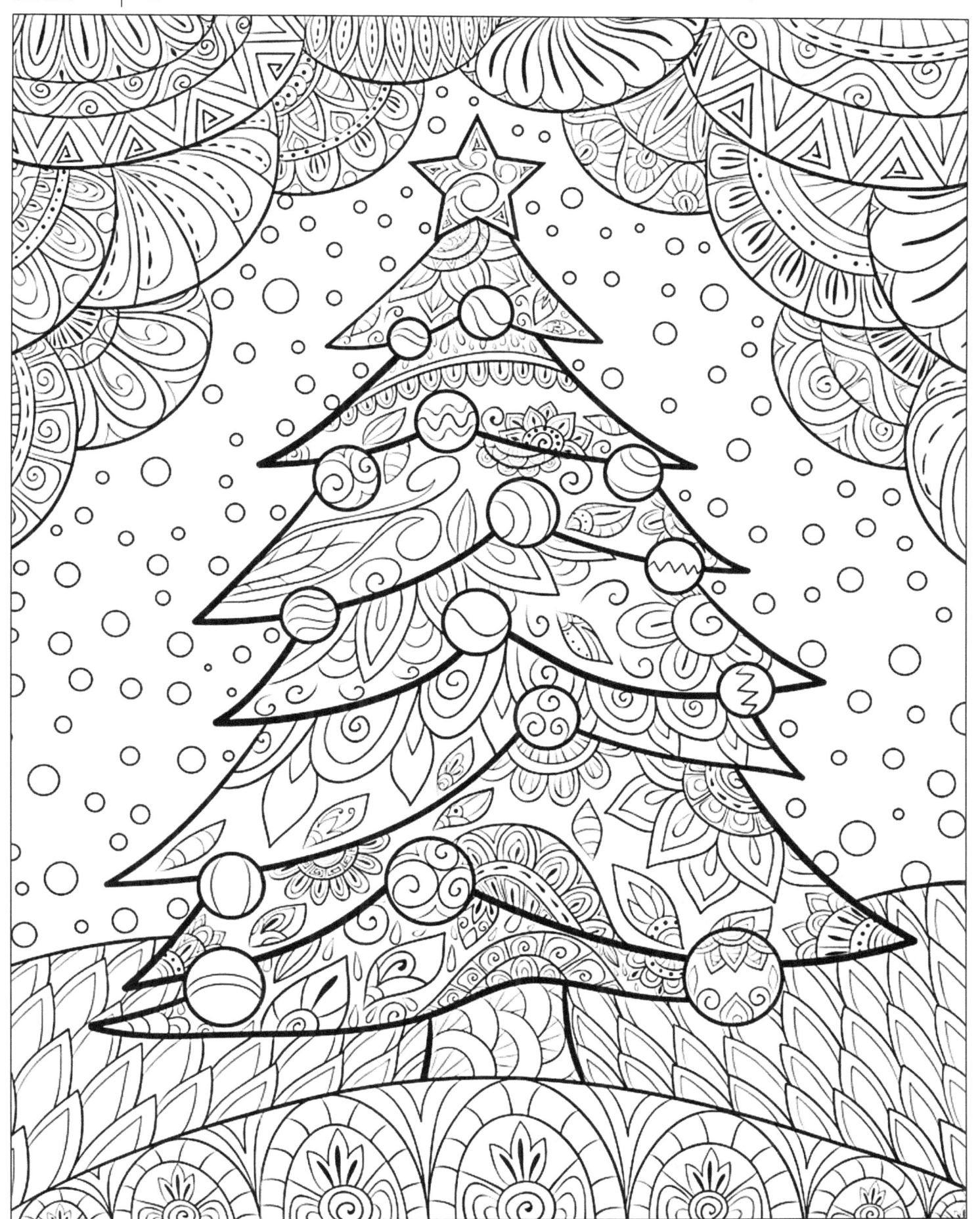

CHRISTMAS CHARM

Page intentionally left withe

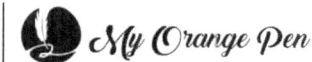

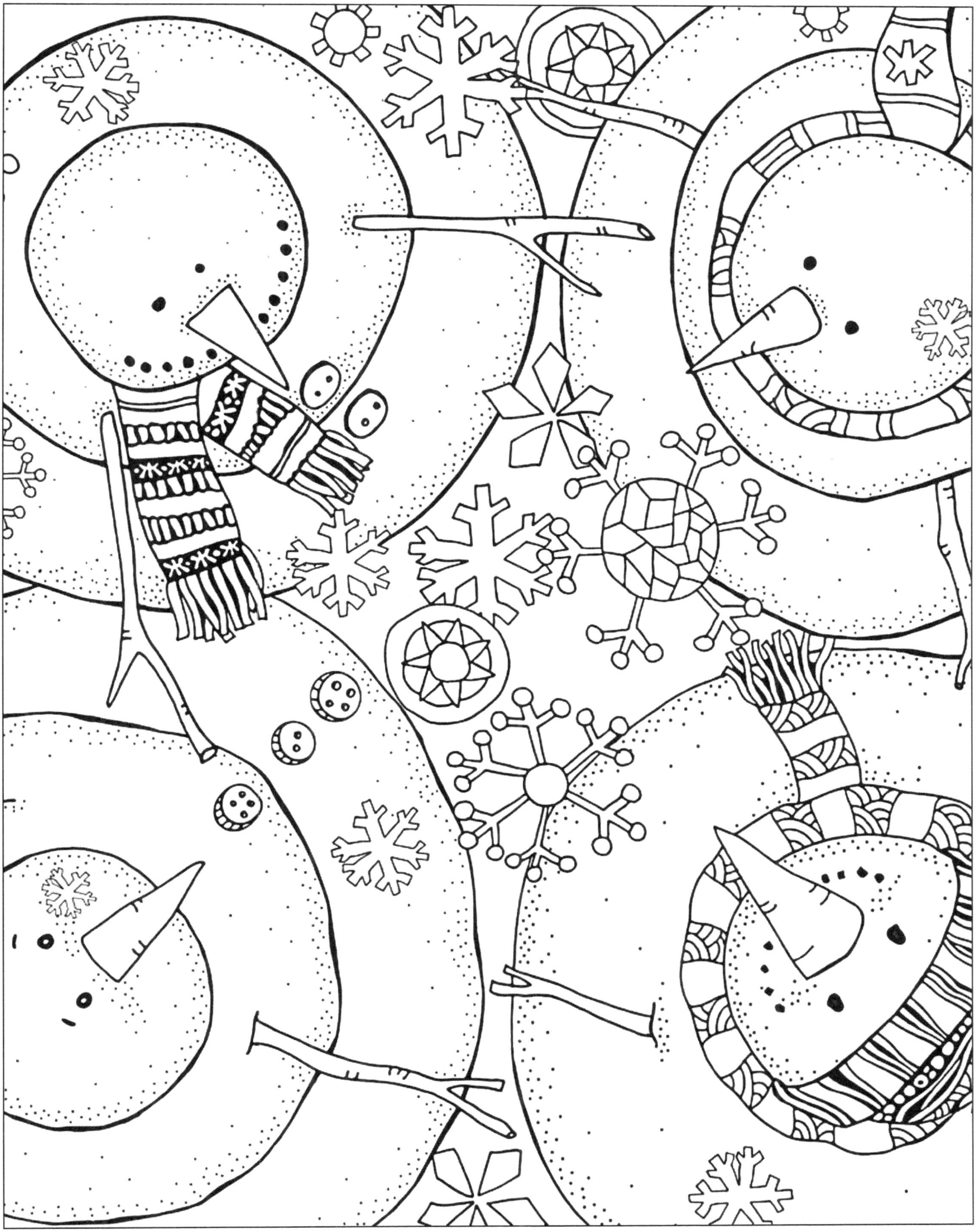

CHRISTMAS CHARM

Page intentionally left withe

CHRISTMAS CHARM

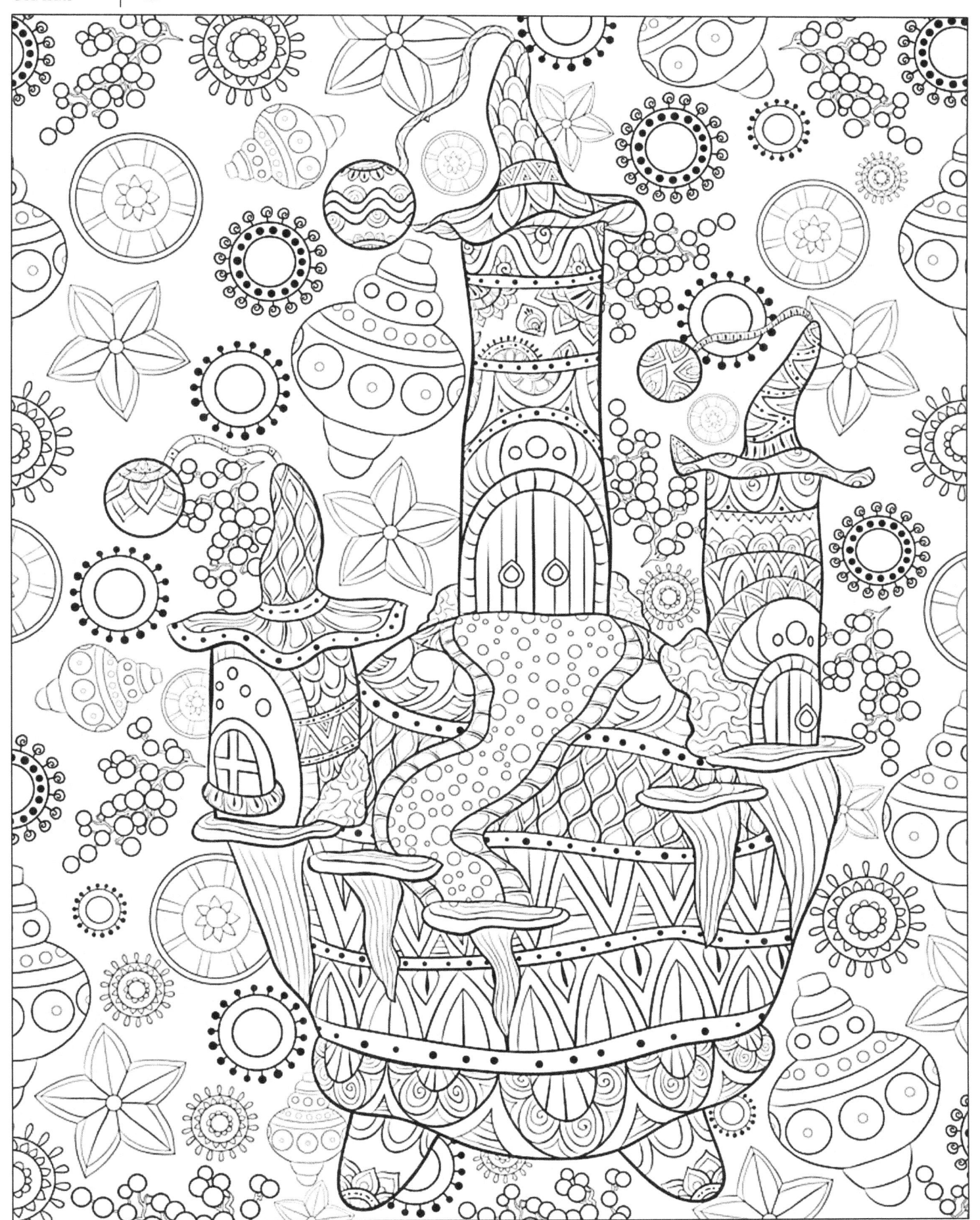

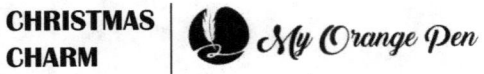

Page intentionally left withe

CHRISTMAS CHARM

Page intentionally left withe

CHRISTMAS CHARM | My Orange Pen

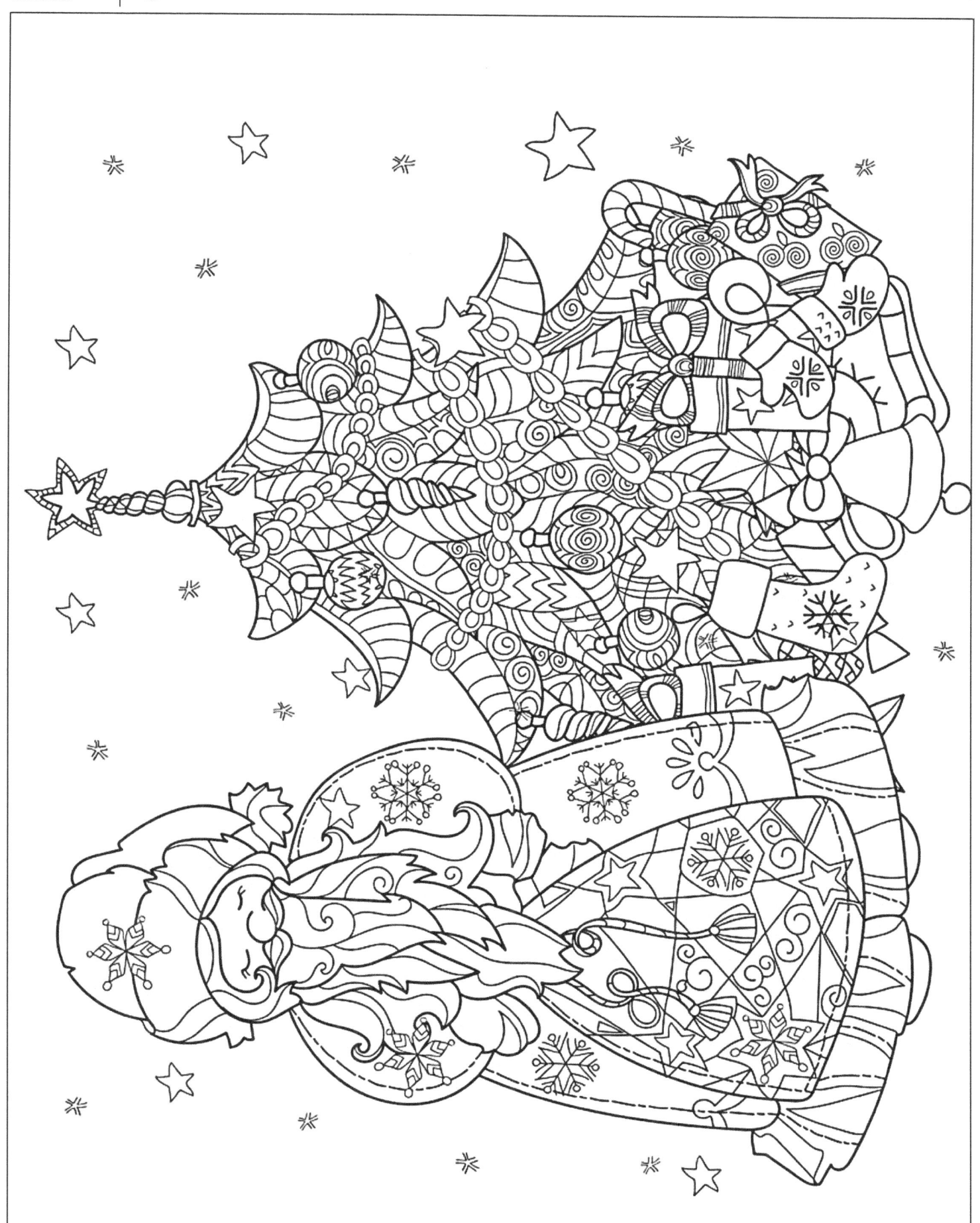

CHRISTMAS CHARM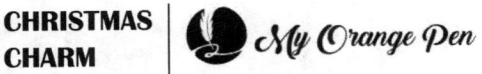

Page intentionally left withe

CHRISTMAS CHARM — My Orange Pen

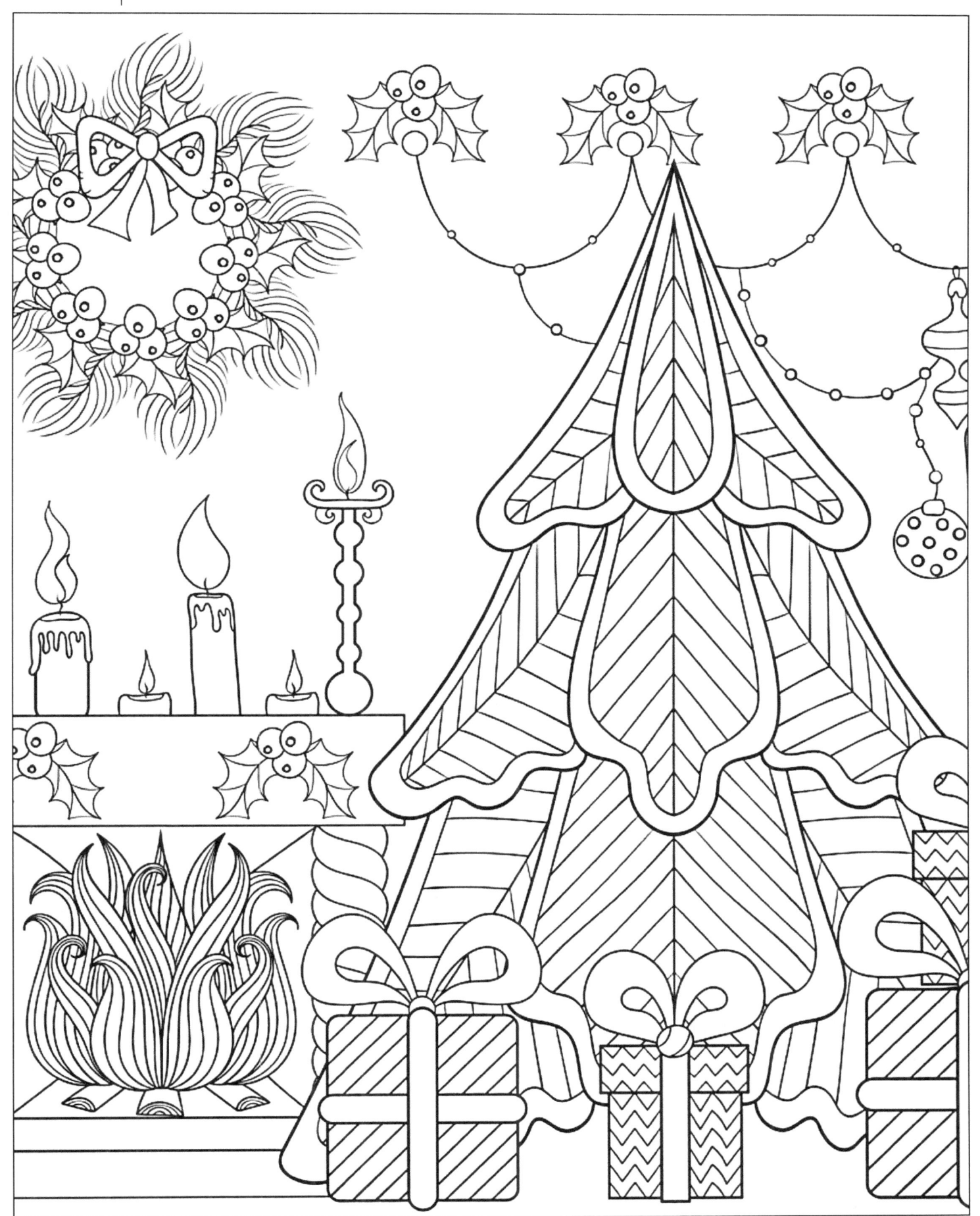

CHRISTMAS CHARM

Page intentionally left withe

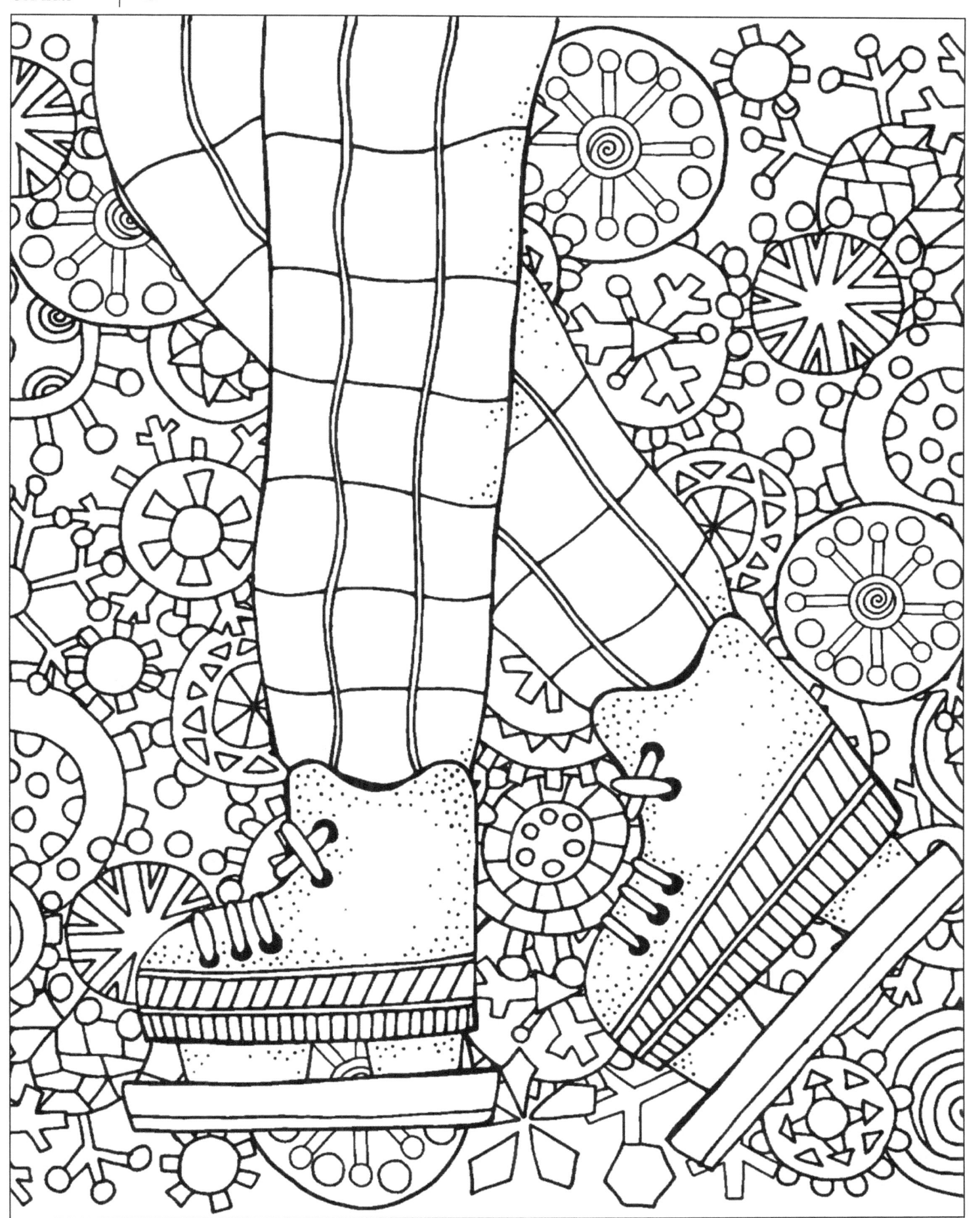

CHRISTMAS CHARM |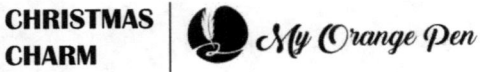

Page intentionally left withe

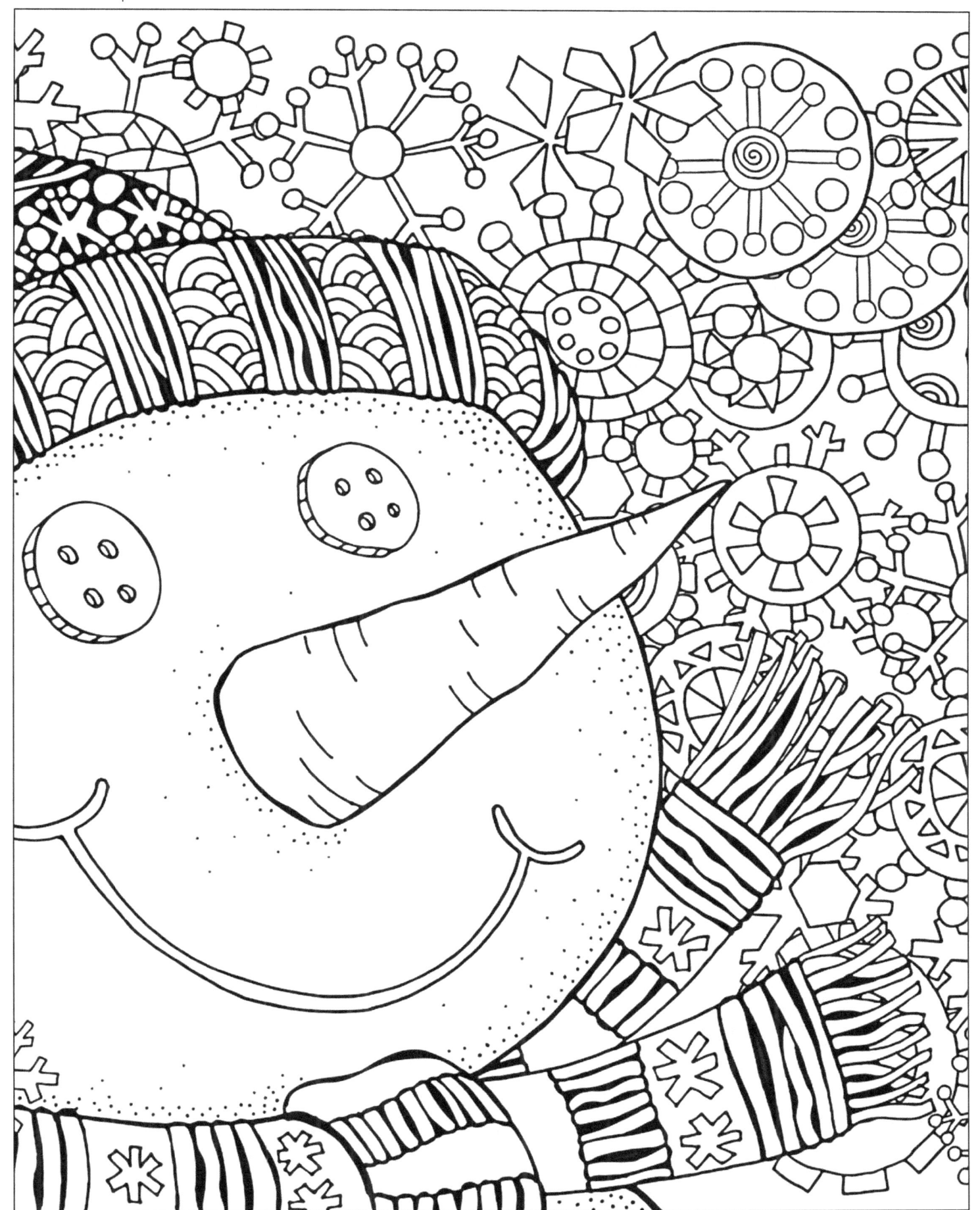

CHRISTMAS CHARM

Page intentionally left with

Don't leave yet without claiming your present! Take your phone and scan the QR code below to get extra 15 drawings for FREE, you can download them and print them as many times as you want!

In the same **X-Mas Collection 2020**

Christmas Charm

ISBN: 9798560431020

Christmas Animals and People

ISBN: 9798561781131

Country Christmas

ISBN: 9798561842962

Christmas Decoration and Ornaments

ISBN: 9798562621597

www.ingramcontent.com/pod-product-compliance
Lightning Source LLC
Chambersburg PA
CBHW080907220526
45466CB00011BA/3501